REBUILDING THE TEMPLE WITHIN YOU

TERRY ADDISON

Rebuilding the Temple Within You

ISBN 1-58169-028-2
For Worldwide Distribution
Printed in the U.S.A.

For further information and availability
please contact:
Terry Addison • c/o Toilers for Jesus Ministries
P.O. Box 741963 • Los Angeles, CA 90004

Table of Contents

Dedication

I want to dedicate this book to my lovely and beautiful wife, Nadia (Nancy). This woman of God believed in me when others turned away, even costing her many friends. Her love, inspiration, gentleness, and patience, has given me the strength and courage to believe that I could do this.

Special Thanks To:

Larry and Rebecca Randolph: They have made such an impact in our lives and where we are today in ministry. For I would not be in ministry today if it had not been for this man of God being obedient to the Holy Spirit on April 22, 1988.

Agnes Numer (Mother Moses): This sweet, sweet woman of God means so much to my wife and I, for she has taught us that the joy of serving is through humility, one to another.

Samuel Callier: This dear man of God birthed within me the importance of holding fast to the anointing within you. It will never lead you astray.

Love you all!

Introduction

It all began in the spring of 1993. I had just finished three weeks of ministering in Indiana, Illinois, and Missouri. I was driving back home to Los Angeles when the Spirit of the Lord came to me saying, "Terry, you are going to be a voice of calmness and peace in the midst of a storm." Now, to be honest with you, at the time I completely ignored those words. I have heard the voice of the Spirit before, and usually, it was to encourage me. A few days later, however, I heard these same words again. Over the next two months, I kept hearing these same words.

But finally after repeating these words once again, He spoke to me and said, "You have been saying, in your prayer time for quite a while, 'I want to be someone You can trust. I want to be someone You can depend on.' Well, I'm saying to you now, are you ready? For Terry, I want to use you for a very special mission which is to warn My Body of the extreme importance of rebuilding their temple within themselves. Why? Because there is a flood coming again. As there was in Noah's day, so shall there even be again."

And I said, "Lord, why me? For I am not one who is articulate, or of great stature in the eyes of many of my peers. I am sure there are many pastors, evangelists, prophets, and teachers who are more worthy than I, and who are far more skilled and knowledgeable in the speech of Your word."

But the Spirit said to me, "What is the name of your ministry?"

I replied, "Toilers for Jesus."

And He said, "Just what exactly does a toiler do?"

I said, "He is a skilled laboring servant who goes about building and instilling within Your family that they need to get excited about who they are in You, letting them know they can live victoriously each and every single day of their lives."

Again the Spirit said to me, "I say unto you now, as I have said to you through My prophets before: You are like David. No one knew anything about him, for he was but a shepherd boy on the back of the desert. But, he was called out, and became one of the greatest kings and leaders Israel has ever known. And have I not also said, you are going to be dynamic voice to this generation? For there is a people who are wounded, who are spoiled, and who have been robbed. And yet, none say 'Restore.' But I have called you to be a restoration man in this generation. because you were willing to go when many would not, for it was not profitable for them, I am advancing you. For I have seen your labor, and know that it is not in vain. For have you not seen the blind see, the deaf hear, the dumb speak, the lame walk, demons flee, diseases of all manner have died again and again as you have used the power and authority which was given unto you in My name?

"I have not chosen you because of your talent. But you were, by many of society's standards totally mentally, physically, and spiritually broken down beyond help. But because of the My grace, and through your humility, I have been able to rebuild you through the Word, physically, mentally, and spiritually. Terry, I charge you that you shall be like as unto Noah, a voice of calmness and peace in the midst of a storm, teaching my family that when the enemy shall come in like a flood, they will be able through the power of the Spirit to set up a standard against him without fear."

In Isaiah 59:19 I believe is the real reason for the rebuilding of our temple which the Lord spoke to me about. It rests solely on one basic principle: Setting up a standard against the wiles of the devil. The strength of the foundation of your temple rests not only on time spent praying, studying, memorizing, and meditating on the Word, but also in understanding the true meaning of the passage: "Greater is He that is in you than he that is in the world."

Begin, begin, begin. Even so, now begin. As I was meditating upon these words, I began to realize that before I could ever begin to understand the importance of the direction it was going to take for them to succeed, that there was an even greater realization that had to take place—that it had to begin with me. The Spirit was desiring me to become an example that He was going to use for His glory.

"What is the purpose of your temple?"

It is a place where you can go

to develop a relationship

one with another

without encountering any opposition.

Chapter I
The Zero Factor

As we begin. Probably the most difficult task that I ever had was giving up control of myself, and so I am sympathetic with anyone who is struggling to do so. I didn't want to let go of me, and just the idea of having someone else in control of my life, well, that was just unthinkable. What if He didn't do things the way I liked? But, you know, God has a unique way of taking some of the simplest situations from our lives and using them to help us through our struggles.

One of these situations occurred when I had been in full-time ministry for a little over four years. This was the first time I had ever taken my ministry outside of the southern California area. On a trip to northern California to visit with my sister-in-law and her family, God opened an opportunity for me to hold a four-day meeting in the Fresno area within a local church. I remember it was early on a Sunday morning that I wanted to spend some time alone in prayer. The meetings weren't scheduled to begin until that evening. My sister-in-law's family was in the business of raising almonds. Right behind their home they had just finished planting their seeds in approximately 40 rows. I must have been walking up and down half of these rows when out of nowhere appeared a cat. This cat followed me up and down five of these rows doing nothing but crying, over and over and over. I tried to scare it away, but failed. Then when I stopped to pick it up, the strangest thing happened—it fell instantly asleep within my arms. Now, this may not seem to be so unusual, but as I continued to walk another four long rows with this cat in my outstretched arms, not one time did this cat ever stir.

All the time I was walking with this cat, God was talking to me. He said, "Terry, take a lesson. You need to become more like this cat in your everyday walk with Me for this cat has totally surrendered itself. It has no fear that you may drop it or harm it in any manner." I cannot tell you how much this lesson means to me, even today, when it comes to learning to surrender yet another part of myself.

It is extremely important we stop right here and really focus in on what the Spirit is saying through this illustration of the cat, and how we can take what He was saying to me and apply it in learning how to daily develop the temple within you. As I look back at that situation in my life now I can see how I almost allowed my own understanding to get in the way of what the Spirit was really trying to accomplish. You see that field I was walking in, even though seeds had been planted, it was still vacant.

That's exactly how we need to look at ourselves as we prepare to build our temples. We are like a vacant lot which has tremendous potential (talents), but as yet there is no foundation. Now we will talk more about this in a few moments, but I want you to understand that it is this lesson which has driven me to seek the Scriptures for the information which I am now sharing with you.

In Hebrews 4:10, God makes reference to the one who has truly learned to enter into the Lord's rest by ceasing from his own:

For he that is entered into his rest, he also hath ceased from his own works, as God did from his.

Why is this so important to God? Because the word *cease* means to stop going in your own direction. For by going in your own direction, you have created an imbalance in your walk. Your flesh is going in one direction, but your spirit man is going in another. How did this happen?

It began by you doing exactly what Proverbs 3:5-6 warned you not to do. You began leaning toward your own understanding, instead of allowing God to direct your path.

Trust in the Lord with all thine heart; and lean not unto thine own understanding. In all thy ways acknowledge him, and he shall direct thy paths.

That's exactly what happened that day with the cat in the field. You see that cat crying out (strange as it may seem) was in all actuality God crying out trying to get my attention, but I was so busy caught up in me walking and talking that I didn't care about anything or anybody else. But thank God this cat (even though I tried to scare it away) never quit crying out. Finally it got my attention, but you know it wasn't until I stopped and picked up that cat that I could actually begin to hear what God was trying to say to me.

With this thought in mind, I wonder how many times God has actually used different situations in your life just to try and get your attention. You know it doesn't have to be a cat, but I believe if you really learn to listen carefully you just might hear Him calling; and if you do, or even if it seems strange, don't ignore it (or send it away)—it just might be God! You must understand you must stop and listen to learn if it is truly God speaking to you.

In Matthew 26:37-40, Jesus gives one of the greatest examples of one who had to stop going in his own direction. This passage talks about Jesus making one of the greatest decisions any man ever made when He made the decision that night in the garden to die. Jesus didn't want to die; He had never done anything wrong—He had never committed a sin. He loved people; He loved life. But He knew He was going to have to die, and it was extremely difficult to handle. Just the thought of the pain He was going to have to go through, must have been unbearable. Three times He rose from praying and went to the church. (Peter, James and John were the church.) What were they doing? They were sleeping.

Now I've often thought about it and have even heard others comment that if the disciples had been awake when Jesus came to them it is quite possible that Jesus would have walked right out of the garden. But because they were asleep when He looked upon them, He saw the sin of man which caused Him to return to praying, saying "Father, not my will, but thine." You see Jesus' work was through. He couldn't go in His own direction. I believe it's important that we look at this with Proverbs 3:5 in mind. God is saying that you must learn to trust Him with *all* your heart. When Jesus died, He did not die because of the nails in his hands or the pain in His side, but He died because of a broken heart. God wants your heart to replace the heart of Jesus which was broken, but unless you can be like Jesus and give Him your all, you haven't given Him anything.

We have such a hard time giving Him our all because we're relying too much upon our own understanding. By doing so, day after day, day after day, what happens is that we create an unbalance in our walk which, in time, can cause us to become narrow minded and only see things a certain way (our way). In reality, what has to happen is that we must desire to become God's favorite number—the number zero. Now if you are like I was, you are probably asking God the same question: "Lord, explain to me just what do you mean by becoming the number zero?" The Lord said, "The world will judge you on a scale from 1 to 10, with 10 being the very best. But did you know, I count backwards? What I mean by that is just let go and let God by learning to die daily to yourself, which can only be accomplished as you learn to forgive yourself of ego, attitude, jealousy, selfishness, bitterness, wrath, malice, violence, anger, temper, haughtiness, and self low esteem."

As Ephesians 4:22 says,

That ye put off concerning the former conversation the old man, which is corrupt according to the deceitful lusts

To become that person whom God is looking for is just not simply desiring to become that zero, but learning to recognize that it is His greatest achievement within you. Now that you have an understanding of what your Lord is actually looking for, I have but one question for you: Are you willing to make the decision to allow God to direct your path? You must become that foundation (start at the very bottom) on which God can begin to rebuild His temple. For, if you can say you are, then let me give you the key to begin. You must STOP.

Chapter II
Understanding Your Importance

You are going to find within this book that I like to ask a lot of questions. My purpose in doing so is that I want to challenge you to look deep within yourself, seeking for an answer. And with that thought in mind, I would like to ask you a question which the Lord asked of me.

At the time, I found this question to be quite puzzling. And still today, after 15 years, in some ways it remains so. But I have found that the more time I spend with my Lord, really getting closer to Him, the more I appreciate who I am in Him. Probably at this moment, many are saying, "But what is the question? Please, tell me." The question is simply: What would it take for the Lord to get your attention to make you feel that you are important to Him? Now, in helping you learn how to answer this, I would like to use myself as an example. It just might be that our thoughts run along the same lines.

I truly believe that the most exciting time in any believer's life is when they have become born again. Well, if you're like I was, my first reaction afterward was, "What happens now?" Even by reading the Word and with my finite understanding, somehow, I got the impression that it was about, "Lord, what can You do for me?" I never considered what I could do for

Him! Much of my talking was this way for about two years, until one day, the Spirit really moved on my life. I have never been the same since!

I had a habit of arriving 30 to 60 minutes early for Sunday evening services. Well, this one evening, I was quite surprised to find that there was no one in the sanctuary except one man, who was a friend. The Spirit spoke to me and said, "Terry, go stand by Ed, for I want to talk with you." As I went and greeted my friend, who was spending some time in reading God's Word, one of the strangest things that I've ever encountered in my life took place. Out of nowhere, this huge eyeball appeared, right in the middle of the Word and winked at us. We just looked at one another, speechless. I had to go sit down. No sooner had I sat down, then the Spirit began speaking to me, and said, "Do you know that I read you as you read Me?" He said, "You read Me to learn from Me, but I read you wanting to know when you are going to let go and enter into the fullness of My Word by clothing yourself with the characteristics and attributes of Jesus, such as meekness, mercy, gentleness, tenderness, kindness, peace, joy, love, compassion, longsuffering, and humility." He said, "Terry, you have been reading My Word for quite some time, and I am pleased, but did you know, My Word talks?"

When thou goest, it shall lead thee; when thou sleepest, it shall keep thee; and when thou awakest, it shall talk with thee (Proverbs 6:22).

"I want to talk with you, for I have been trying to get your attention, but you're always so busy. I want you to understand that you are important, and I need you to do nothing but sit down and listen to what I'm saying. It's going to take some time to prepare you properly for your calling—your holy calling."

> . . .*according to the power of God; who has saved us and called us with a holy calling* (2 Timothy 1:8-9).

"My Word says in Romans 12:2 that you need to renew the mind, and Terry, you need it badly."

> *And be not conformed to this world: but be ye transformed by the renewing of your mind, that ye may prove what is that good, and acceptable, and perfect will of God* (Romans 12:2).

"For you have gotten so caught up in yourself with this stinkin' thinkin,' that if you think wrong about yourself, then you're going to believe wrong. If you believe wrong, then you're going to speak wrong. If you speak wrong, then you're going to act wrong. And if your actions are wrong, then your results are going to be wrong. And it all began with that stinkin' thinkin.' So many of my children are just like Adam and Eve were when they hid themselves from Me in the Garden, and I had to look for them. They just weren't aware of their importance."

Did you know that the Spirit is saying today that it is an absolute honor to be called on by God? Do you understand the importance of that statement? Out of all the people He could call on, He wants you. Why? Because He wants to bless you. He believes in you so much that He can trust you, even with His Word (His life). But you know, there are so many who are still saying, "I hope He doesn't call on me." You know, they are just like those Israelites who were told to take the promised land, but saw themselves only as grasshoppers because of the giants there. In Proverbs 23:7, it says, "as a man thinketh in his heart, so is he." It's saying, if that's how you see yourself, then that's how you believe you will become. But you need to begin to see yourself as God sees you. And God does not see you the way you are, but He sees you the way the Word says you are. And the Word says you are:

Romans 5:1—*justified*. When the Lord looks upon you, He does not see you. He sees the blood, as if you had never sinned.

Acts 26:18—*sanctified*. You are being set apart for special use.

Proverbs 4:6—*preserved*. You are being kept safe from harm or injury.

Ephesians 1:3—*blessed*. All the riches of His glory have have been bestowed upon you.

1 Peter 2:9—*chosen*. You are valued highly.

Romans 5:17 (Amplified Bible)—*royalty*. You are called as kings, to rule and reign in this life.

Ephesians 1:7—*redeemed*. You have been bought with a great price, the blood of His own Son.

Romans 8:16—*joint-heir*. You have the right to inherit. All that's been given unto Jesus has been given unto you.

Ephesians 2:6—*citizens of heaven*. You are seated with Him in heavenly places.

Colossians 2:10—*complete in Him*. You lack nothing.

As believers, you have been given, as it says in Genesis 1:26, dominion (the right and the power to govern and control) over everything on this earth. As our fine brother Charles Capps would say, "You even have dominion over all creeps." In Luke 10:19, you are told that you have been given power and authority over all the power of the enemy, and not to fear. I believe God is looking for Davids, others like that man of courage. David did not see himself as a grasshopper when he came up against Goliath, but as a giant-killer. Not only did he defeat and kill him, but he cut his head off! We need to take note of this. For, by cutting off the head of every foul, evil, lying demon that you are going to come up against, you are cutting off all intimidation. Never again can they bother you. So, don't just speak to them, put them in their place. Put them under your feet.

Once again, I want to challenge you to look deep within yourself, because, before we can take that next important step and continue on in our next lesson, there is something you need to recognize. He's calling, just as He did with Adam and Eve, and before you can ever turn this page, He is waiting for someone to answer. The question is, will you?

Chapter III
Project-Temple: Knowledge Accumulation of Facts

Diligence: A constant steady effort to achieve.

How's your memory? I am sure that if you concentrate hard enough that you can remember an experience which you've had in your life that can relate to the word, *diligent*, and the effort which it took for you to achieve your goal. I want you to think about this experience because you must prepare yourself for the extreme challenge you are going to face in the rebuilding of your temple. Why?

I believe that we are living today in a world where anything goes, just like the city of Las Vegas. That reminds me of the apostle Paul and his journey into Corinth when he tried to bring the Word of God into a society where they worshiped the goddess Diana. I believe that one of the most difficult responsibilities in society today is to be a believer. For, in many cases, it is not very popular to be a Christian. To be honest with you, I really can't put all the blame on those who are lost. I believe that we, as Christians, have failed in many instances to carry on the ministry of our Lord and Savior. Why?

Because so many believers have not taken a stand, it has caused much of the world to seek after other religions, such as Mormonism, Buddhism, Hinduism, Humanism, Secularism, Satanism, even "T.V.-ism." I can share about this because I am a former Jehovah's Witness. For 7-1/2 years, I was totally sold out to this movement. A few years back, the Lord gave me a "whipping" in the closet during my prayer time like never before. You see, I was always complaining (or so it seemed) about seeing the Jehovah's Witnesses out in our area going door to door. I was totally shocked by the response which I got from the Lord. He said, "How dare you stand there and complain about them being out there winning all those people." He said, "They're winning them because you're surely not doing anything, now are you? Where are you? You're not being an example for Me."

From this, I began to learn the importance of getting involved in the world. There are not as many believers in the world today as they say there are. If there were, then their walk would show it. Many of the lost would recognize it and want to know, "What makes you so different?" If you just so happened to be involved in the word, then you would be able to help them, right?"

I'm sure there are some who are saying, "I thought this book was about the rebuilding of *our* temple." But, before this can begin to take place, we have to understand the areas of our lives which need correction, and the proper procedures with which to handle them.

Family, there must be an agreement that your involvement is not going to be one in the actual building. Your involvement is going to be in learning how to give of yourself, allowing God to use you for His glory.

Knowledge

Believers in general today, really don't understand what it truly means to be led by the Spirit. Now, in 1 John 2:27, the Bible says,

But the anointing which ye have received of him abideth in you, and ye need not that any man teach you: but as the same anointing teacheth you of all things, and is truth, and is no lie, and even as it hath taught you, ye shall abide in him.

I believe that this passage, in all actuality, is an absolute confirmation that the Spirit has to become the teacher if we are ever going to learn how to become victorious in our everyday lives.

Now, as we look at Proverbs 24:3-4, I truly believe this is going to be the direction we are going to be taking in the development of our temple. What seems to be very different is the manner in which the Lord ministered the importance of these words to me—He taught me these passages in reverse order.

Through wisdom is a house builded; and by understanding it is established: and by knowledge shall the chambers be filled with all precious and pleasant riches.

Now, the main words He wanted me to focus on were: knowledge (the accumulation of facts), understanding (the ability to arrange the facts), and wisdom (the ability to apply the facts). In gaining God's knowledge, there has to be the desire on your part to spend time with Him. It just can't be an occasional moment when you feel like it. For if you really desire His heart, then it is very simple. You have to learn what it means to sacrifice yourself, recognizing that the Bible is just not any ordinary book, but it is, in all actuality, the Word of God, and that it changes lives. As we learned in the last chapter, this Word actually talks, and what's even more exciting than that, is to know that He wants to talk just with you (Proverbs 6:22).

I guarantee you, that if you allow His Word to talk with you, that you will learn more in 5 minutes than if you were to sit and read it for 5 hours. In Proverbs 4:20-22, the Scriptures say,

My son, attend to my words; incline thine ear unto my sayings. Let them not depart from thine eyes; keep them in the midst of thine heart. For they are life unto those that find them, and health to all their flesh.

These words need to become so real to you that you can't stay away from them or want to put them down because they are alive. I honestly believe that, the more time you spend in the Word, the more often miracles can happen, and are happening, in your life and many other believers' lives today. Why? Because you're making yourself available to Him.

Now, I know we are talking about knowledge, but I honestly feel we need to put more focus on this word, *miracle*. For, I can tell you, being in fellowship meetings and hearing of the many miracles which have taken place in people's lives, has given me the strength to begin believing it for myself, saying, "Hey, why not me?" I would like to share with you a few miracles which have taken place in my life. I know that there are many believers, and even non-believers, who have done things in their lives, or have been in situations, where they just felt like there was no way God could ever forgive or want to use them. The things which have happened in my life prove that belief is false.

Let it be known, I am a miracle, and this is not ego-speaking. For 30 years of my life, I considered myself an illiterate. I was adopted at about the age of 5 and lived in a home for 16 years where I was told almost every single day by my step-parents, "Boy, you're never going to amount to anything." And, do you know what? I began to believe it. It took me 14 years to get through high school, and then they just passed me on, for 95 percent of my grades were failing. I was even voted by my classmates the most unlikely to succeed at anything I would ever do. Well, that almost became a reality when a few years later I was living in Los Angeles and had lost my job and everything I owned. Suddenly I found myself living on the streets of skid row, which I did for a little over 2 years. I could go on, for there have been many miracles since, but my purpose in sharing this is to encourage you, and let you know, that you too can be a testimony for Jesus.

We have talked extensively and have made a great number of references about the importance of getting into the word. I don't want to seem as though I'm repeating myself so often, but I want you to get this into your spirits, so that it becomes real. Your hearts are the keys to your "project temple." Remember what the Lord says at the end of the passage of Proverbs 16:1,

> *The preparations of the heart in man, and the answer of the tongue, is from the Lord.*

The answer of the tongue—notice, it is your tongue. But also recognize the statement is from the Lord. For this statement is in reference to how much of the Word is within you. It is important to grasp. God can only speak through you according to the degree of knowledge (accumulation of facts) within you. If you have just a small portion of the Word in you, then that is all He can build upon.

Family, I want to challenge you to become diligent, every single day of your lives, in the preparation of your hearts. That the direction of your paths made up of your footsteps, has finally replaced your own understanding, by your coming to recognize that you just can't live without Him, you've just got to have Him.

Chapter IV
Project-Temple:
Understanding
Ability to Arrange the Facts

In 1 John 1:5, the Word says this is the message that God is light, and in Him, there is no darkness. Briefly, we spoke in the previous chapters of the importance today in becoming a witness. In order for you to be effective, your life must be based upon what light does.

I believe that this passage is in direct reference to what the condition the nation of Israel was like during Jesus' ministry. We must realize that from the end of the book of Malachi to the appearing of John the Baptist at the Jordan River was approximately 420-430 years in which God had not spoken to the nation of Israel because of the hardness of their hearts. They had turned from the teachings of Moses unto legalism, or Judaism (the law of the Elders). In today's society, it is no different. Religion is nothing more than what man says God is all about. But, the Gospel (Good News) is who God says He is, and they are as different as light and darkness. That's why today, it is not only important for believers to have that understanding of the Word, which can be found in Psalm 119:169, but for true growth to become effective, it can only happen through meditating (on the law of the Lord) or the Word of the Lord, "Both day and night" (Psalm 1:2).

In Psalm 119:130, we read "The entrance of the Word gives light." I would like to propose a question: Doesn't light reveal? I believe it is important that we understand that this light not only refers to giving you direction, but the Lord is wanting to get you excited about the Word becoming *alive* within you. In Ephesians 1:18, we read, "the eyes of your understanding." Now, when I first read this, the Spirit spoke to me and said, "Don't pass this up, did you get that?" I replied, "Get what, Father?" He said, "Terry, understanding has eyes."

Previously, we studied that knowledge was nothing more than hearing what the Word had to say by letting it talk. So then, we also, through the understanding of His eyes, can now begin to see not only His direction for our lives, but that we also have real purpose. Each and every single day, we learn to trust Him more by giving of ourselves unto His Word unconditionally, which, in all finality, brings us exactly to where the Lord really wanted us to begin with—in that personal relationship (that oneness) just you and Him.

In Romans 1:17, we read, "The just shall live by faith." Now, when I talk about faith, I am not talking about man's kind of faith, which relates mostly to "blab it and grab it" or "name it and claim it" conversation. But I am talking about a gift from God which was given unto every man, woman, and child who have received Jesus as their personal Lord and Savior, that we may begin to have an understanding, that we are called to a higher and quality type of life, and "to let your moderation be made known to all men" (Philippians 1:5).

Family, I want to challenge you to have the faith and to take hold of the understanding that so many of our brothers and sisters had who went on before us, such as in Hebrews 11:

Understanding

5 By faith Enoch was translated that he should not see death; and was not found, because God had translated him: for before his translation he had this testimony, that he pleased God.

7 By faith Noah, being warned of God of things not seen as yet, moved with fear, prepared an ark to the saving of his house; by the which he condemned the world, and became heir of the righteousness which is by faith.

8 By faith Abraham, when he was called to go out into a place which he should after receive for an inheritance, obeyed; and he went out, not knowing whither he went.

9 By faith he sojourned in the land of promise, as in a strange country, dwelling in tabernacles with Isaac and Jacob, the heirs with him of the same promise:

20 By faith Isaac blessed Jacob and Esau concerning things to come.

21 By faith Jacob, when he was a dying, blessed both the sons of Joseph; and worshiped, leaning upon the top of his staff.

24 By faith Moses, when he was come to years, refused to be called the son of Pharaoh's daughter;

27 By faith he forsook Egypt, not fearing the wrath of the king: for he endured, as seeing him who is invisible.

29 By faith they passed through the Red sea as by dry land: which the Egyptians assaying to do were drowned.

19

30 By faith the walls of Jericho fell down, after they were compassed about seven days.

31 By faith the harlot Rahab perished not with them that believed not, when she had received the spies with peace.

33 who through faith subdued kingdoms, wrought righteousness, obtained promises, stopped the mouths of lions,

13 These all died in faith, not having received the promises, but having seen them afar off, and were per-suaded of them, and embraced them, and confessed that they were strangers and pilgrims on the earth.

For like those who went on before us, and saw the promises afar off, you also now have all these promises at hand, right here in the Word.

In Psalm 50:23, the Word says, "order your conversation." Did you catch that? It says you have the ability to arrange and order what comes out of your mouth before you even speak. Why? Because your mouth is subject to the spirit within you. Also, notice what you have received in 1 Corinthians 2:12,

Now we have received, not the spirit of the world, but the Spirit which is of God; that we might know the things that are freely given to us of God.

More than anything else, I believe the Lord wants to see in you exactly what He said He saw in me: the greatness which is within each and every single one of you. But one question still remains. Just what does your light do?

Chapter V
Project-Temple:
Wisdom
Ability to Apply the Facts

Proverbs 4:7- Wisdom is the principal thing.

I grew up in the small mid-western town of Summitville, Indiana, surrounded by a vast expanse of farms. I have had many opportunities to hear conversations amongst the farmers themselves about what they believed their crop was going to do during a particular year. What amazed me the most was, how much they believed in what they were saying. They were absolutely convinced that the seeds they had planted were going to produce great rows of corn, wheat, oats, beans, or whatever it was they had sowed. The lives of their families depended solely on their belief, and that's exactly how this Word of God must become in your life. There are going to be many difficult situations you are going to be facing in your life, whether it is the need of a job, getting married, a financial problem, or even a health problem. You must come to believe that the words which you are speaking are not just mere words, but they are like the mustard seed, which, when planted properly, grows up and becomes greater than any situation the devil may be trying to drop on you. Mark 4:31-32 says,

21

It is like a grain of mustard seed, which, when it is sown in the earth, is less than all the seeds that be in the earth: but when it is sown, it groweth up, and becometh greater than all herbs, and shooteth out great branches; so that the fowls of the air may lodge under the shadow of it.

You know, many times during my ministry, God has actually taken me to events just to let me learn that we, as a body of believers, are not doing enough for His kingdom. I can recall one time when I was in the city of San Francisco, out of nowhere I heard loud music and people yelling. It turned out to be a parade like none I'd ever seen before. It was an event for gay rights. There must have been almost 5,000 people involved in this movement carrying signs, singing, dancing, and yelling, all for their cause. I said, "Lord, would you look at this? It almost makes you want to cry. That they can gather that many people together for their cause, and we have such a hard time getting five people together just to witness. It's an absolute shame." But the Spirit spoke to me and said, "Take notice, for there is not one person who seems to be ashamed of what they're doing or saying, just as there is no shame in the world today amongst those who have taken a stand for abortion, racism, and the occult, and believe it is all right. You see, they have a real problem, because they have become so addicted to evil that their own tongues have become their own worst enemies (they are condemned by the words of their own mouth).

America belongs to Jesus, and the Spirit is looking for the ones today who are unashamed, and who will stand up and do what Jeremiah 33:11 says we are to do: "lift up that voice of joy and gladness by restoring that voice of praise (spoken

22

word) into the house of God." As this is done, not only will the captive land be restored, but marriages, families, jobs, and health as well.

God is looking today for a wise person, and I would like to share with you a passage, which at first, I found to be quite strange, but in the end, turned out to teach me a great lesson. This passage is found in Proverbs 6:6. It says, "[Consider] the ant thou sluggard . . . and be wise." I believe this verse is talking about your relationship with the Lord and the quality time which you really need to spend with Him. Why? Because, have you ever sat down and watched an ant? He is always busy—busy building. Never does he have to be told what to do. In Proverbs 6:9, it goes on to ask, how long are you going to continue to sleep? When are you going to wake up and do something? If you really love the Lord as much as you say, then that should be more than enough to drive you to become more like that watchman: always busy learning, meditating and building, never one to be known as a sluggard, but one who is wise.

Today, the devil is on a rampage like never before, but I believe much of that is due to many believers (people of action) who are doing absolute damage to his worldly kingdom. I want to encourage you (if you are one of those), don't let up! For you see, that's exactly the same problem the devil was having with Jesus in Mark 4:35-40. You see, the devil actually thought that it was a perfect time to make his move. He was thinking, "Now Jesus is tired, for He has been ministering almost all day. Now it is night time, and He's taking His pillow and getting on the boat along with His disciples to get some rest. What a great time to create a storm and take care of them all at once." And you know, for a moment it worked, because the disciples panicked so badly that when they went to Jesus, they actually accused Him of not caring. How many times have you missed it in your life and blamed Jesus when it was really the devil? But I want you to notice what Jesus does. He doesn't panic, but He arises, rebukes the wind, and says to the sea, "Peace. Be still." and it was so. Now the disciples were so amazed, that they even began talking among themselves, "What manner of man is this, that even the winds and the sea obey?"

Now I believe that it's extremely important for you to take note of what the disciples said. They made mention of the word *man*. Why is this so important? Because they themselves were just men. Why didn't one of them stand up and say something? Now I just know that there are some of you who are thinking, "Wait a minute, this is not just any ordinary man. This is Jesus." But there's something you need to understand. Jesus may have been all God, but He was also all man. His purpose in coming to earth was not to minister as a Son of God, but as a Son of man. That's why I will always continue to say, they (the disciples) may not have been Jesus, but they could have done what He did, and I will prove this through the Word.

Before we go on any further, I want to make mention of what Jesus actually says to His disciples: "How is it you have no faith?" For this is the key to the whole text. Please let me explain. In 2 Corinthians 4:8-10, this passage is talking about the fact that even though you may be perplexed, distressed, troubled, or persecuted, you must will allow the life of Jesus to come alive within you, to take hold of you, and allow it to grow within you. Do not look to your circumstances nor your situations which surround you, then you will begin to see that you do have the same spirit of faith which Jesus did on that day. Without any fear, if you believe, you can begin to speak

24

that word, and know, beyond a shadow of a doubt, it shall be so (2 Corinthians 4:13).

We having the same spirit of faith, according as it is written, I believed, and therefore have I spoken; we also believe, and therefore speak.

For the Word says that,

...so shall my word be that goeth forth. It shall not return unto me void, but accomplish, please, and prosper whereto I sent it (Isaiah 55:11).

Note: Faith receives the moment it believes it receives.

Yes, wisdom is a principle thing (first in importance). But I want to challenge you to become more like that farmer, absolutely convinced. And, oh, yes, his job may seem to be simple to many, but recognize that nothing is ever gained if nothing has ever been planted (Word applied). So you see, it takes work. I guess the next step then is to get off your seat, right?

Chapter VI

Off Your Seat
Onto Your Feet
Into the Street

12 Verily, verily, I say unto you, He that believeth on me, the works that I do shall he do also; and greater *works* than these shall he do; because I go unto my Father.

Developing Toilers
to
Reach Out
And
Touch Someone

Soldiers of God, attention! I am your friendly drill instructor, and I have been instructed by the Holy Spirit to begin training you in the areas and the joy(s) of witnessing. And please let it be made known, to everyone, that this is not just some course which you can take to see if you might like it or not. But this is a direct order, and as a believer, you are commanded to do it (John 14:12).

In beginning, you must first understand that God's training of His servants, even though it may be similar to the training of soldiers in our armed forces today, is really quite different. As their training revolves around preparing for *physical* battle, your training is going to revolve around doing *spiritual* battle by pulling down strongholds, casting down imaginations, etc. (2 Corinthians 10:4-5).

for the weapons of our warfare are not carnal, but mighty through God to the pulling down of strongholds casting down imaginations, and every high thing that exalteth itself against the knowledge of God, and bringing into captivity every thought to the obedience of Christ...

You must also become aware that to be a true servant of God is to be one who is not only willing to be taught, but one who is teachable. As true servants, you are going to be tested; and many times, the devil will use your own family, friends, co-workers, and classmates to do just that.

I must admit that one of my greatest fears was witnessing, and it wasn't until the Spirit used one of my favorite pastimes to teach me differently, that I even considered the seriousness of witnessing. Let me explain. I used to enjoy sitting and watching old war movies by the hours. One evening the Spirit just spoke to me and said, "Who do you believe is the most important person out of all those men charging up the hill?" I replied, "The man who's leading the charge." He said, "It would seem to be that way, wouldn't it? But it's the man with the radio, because he is trained to survey the situation and then radio back to the warplanes and warships where to place the bombs. For the lives of all those men depend upon that man, not only relaying his message properly, but for those also on the receiving end knowing his voice. For you see, over the hill is an unknown territory, and they can't advance until it's absolutely safe to do so. The timing has to be right."

In John 10:4, Jesus says, "my sheep follow me because they know my voice." In witnessing, one of the worst mistakes that I ever made, and I'm sure there have been others like me, was saying, "Oh, well. There's always tomorrow. I've got plenty of time." Until one evening, the Spirit spoke to me very gently, and said, "My son, what if there were no tomorrow?" I said, "Lord, I have no answers for you except I'm sorry." And I started weeping uncontrollably, saying "Lord, give me another chance. Please let me have another tomorrow." And He said, "But that's the problem, my son. The heart of man has become a heart of tomorrow." I must have relived that night a thousand times over, but it changed me. Listen! You cannot be a true soldier of God today, and have the heart of God unless you are a soldier who has a burden for souls.

Onto Your Feet

From the Scriptures, I would like to share with you real

28

witnesses of God who had the qualities of that soldier I believe the Lord is looking for today, such as:

Abraham—man of faith, Genesis 13:14-17.

Now I'm sure that wherever Abraham looked that day—whether it was to the north, south, east, or west—all he saw was nothing but vacant land. And if he would have waited for a sign from God before he moved, he would have waited forever.

God told him to arise and go. I truly believe that all God was looking for was someone to believe in Him and take Him at His word.

Delight thyself also in the Lord; and he shall give thee the desires of thine heart (Psalm 37:4).

I would like for you to notice the word *desire*, for it means the beginning of achieving. But wisdom is in knowing that you can't achieve anything by standing still. I said that because there are believers today who are saying, "Lord, give me a sign so that I know it's you, then I'll move." When all he's really looking for is that Abraham who will take Him at His word and begin.

Moses—man of courage, a synopsis of Exodus 2-11.

Think about this. Here is a man who was in a position of power and wealth in the country of Egypt, but because he committed a murder, he had to flee into the desert to Midian. In the desert, he had a conversation with his creator, standing in the presence of the burning bush. Now I believe that on that day, not only did Moses come to understand the real heart of God, but he actually heard the cries coming from the nation of

Israel. With his new-found courage, power, and love, he then understood his calling. It was through that calling, in which he received his strength, that he was able to come out from the desert of Midian once again to the land of Egypt (2 Timothy 1:9). On ten different occasions, he went into the presence of Pharaoh, demanding, "Let my people go." Moses was neither moved by what he saw nor by what he heard in Pharoah's court. Rather, he chose to stand upon the Word of God with courage, until the victory came.

Daniel—man of humility, a synopsis of Daniel 1-11.

So many times we go through experiences in our lives, wondering "How could God allow this to happen?" But all He's really doing is testing your dedication to your calling. For that's exactly what He was doing with Daniel, who had become a prisoner. The nation of Israel had been taken captive during the reign of Jehoakim, king of Babylon.

On three different occasions, Daniel is called upon to interpret the dreams of Nebuchadnezzar with the end result being that Daniel found favor with the king.

On another occasion, because Daniel refuses to obey the decree (that no one was to pray) he is thrown into the lions' den. Even in light of this situation, Daniel chose rather to draw near unto his God by humbling himself (James 4:10). Now I need to repeat something here, for you need to grasp the importance of this. Here was a man who was a prisoner, and because of his humility, he was favored above all presidents and princes because an excellent spirit was seen in him (Daniel 6:3).

Today, soldier of God, what does He see in you, excuses or confidence? I have tried to present three types of witnesses, but do you know what's most unique about these situations? In each one, He used just one single person. What's stopping you from stepping forward and becoming that one as well? He is waiting.

Into the Street

Soldier of God, my desire in sharing so many illustrations (as I'm about to do once again) is that you may learn from the mistakes of those before you and how to correct them.

Early in my ministry, I was involved with Youth For Christ. One of the responsibilities I had was in working with the youth in the street ministry. Now, there was a young man who had been coming for quite some time to the meetings, and we knew he hadn't received the Lord as yet. So, one of the leaders went to a young brother in the Lord who was quite popular and who seemed to enjoy witnessing, and said, "Brother, I'm having some difficulty in sharing with this one young man. Would you do me a favor and help me out? He seems to have a lot of respect for you." Now, instead of this brother going to this young man, he passed on the responsibility to someone else, who in turn, did likewise as well. This went on for about two weeks, and still, no one had taken the time to speak with him. One week later, he passed away.

Why did I share this? Because, if there is anyone whom God is looking for today, it is a person who understands responsibility. Not just in the sense of witnessing to lost souls, but one who is responsible in knowing, understanding, and using the weapons he has been given.

A soldier in the armed forces is taught to know his weapon so well that he can take it apart and put it back together again blindfolded, because it is his protection. And soldier of God, you must not only know your weapon, but it is absolutely essential that you understand that lives are so important to God that He can't just trust anyone. Think about this. If He cannot use you, then tell me, who can He use? For you are all He has.

I would like to share with you a passage which the Lord shared with me in reference to the proper procedures a soldier of God is required to learn. It is found in Psalm 32:8.

I will instruct thee and teach thee in the way which thou shalt go: I will guide thee with mine eye.

As I was meditating on this verse, the Lord spoke to me and said, "Terry, do you know that the most important responsibility of the Holy Spirit today is to serve you? He wants to be your servant. Now when it comes to the area of witnessing, He wants you to understand that the key is to send the Spirit out before you. By doing so, He goes out and surveys the land (unknown territory) so He knows when to move, where to move, and when not to move."

Soldier of God, it's vitally important that you learn the meaning of patience (standing fast). For when it's time for you to move, He will let you know. And understand, you won't just be going out, but you will be walking in the footsteps of the Spirit, who went before you.

The end result is the absolute joy of raiding the enemies' camp and returning that loved one once again to his heavenly father, and to hear those words, "Well done, my good and faithful servant."

So I say to you today, Soldier of God, off your seat, onto your feet! Attack! Attack! Attack!

Chapter VII
The Urgency of the Moment
(Call to Prayer)

I believe that the word *urgency* is a word taken for granted by many in our society today who have never come to realize the real importance of it until it is too late.

To be honest with you, for a long time that's exactly how I treated my whole walk with my Lord. Now, up to this time in my life, I have probably spent 20 years in church, rarely missing a service. Everything I did was taken for granted. My purpose in going to church wasn't to learn (even though I believed I was), but to be seen. To say, "See, I told you I was a Christian. I even brought my Bible." I would give my one dollar a week and believe I was doing something great for His kingdom. I wasn't a believer, I was a make-believer, until an urgency of the moment hit me right between the eyes. I'll never forget that day, for it turned out to be the most glorious day I have ever experienced.

It was in Los Angeles, California, on November 30, 1979, at 4:30 p.m. My wife and I were on our way home from work. Traffic was horrendous. It was bumper to bumper for miles, both in front of us and behind. We were located in the slow lane at the bottom of the entrance ramp leading to the San Bernardino freeway. My foot was on the brake, and my wife had a bowl in her lap, relaxing and waiting for the traffic to move. As well as I remember it (for it all happened so fast), I heard a siren, and I believe that someone was running from the police, and by accident, drove onto the entrance ramp, believing it was a side street. They must have been going fast because my wife only had time to look up and yell, "Oh, God! Help!" I tried to move over in the lane, but I must have reacted so fast and turned the steering wheel so hard, that my hands just slipped off. The momentum carried my hands, head, and shoulders out the driver's side window. The car went over three lanes, ending right next to the center divider. Something literally picked me up and put me back in my seat, facing straight ahead. I didn't know why at that moment, but I was weeping profusely.

I knew something had happened, but I couldn't explain it. And please don't misunderstand me, but it was as though I became instantly super-intelligent. But now I realize what really happened was that I became alive to the spirit within me. My first impression on looking at the front windshield was one of total shock. For the car in front of me must have been ten car lengths ahead. I glanced down at my speedometer and I was doing 55 miles per hour. What happened? For just ten seconds before, I was sitting three lanes over in bumper to bumper traffic. How did I get here? Why didn't I hit somebody? How did I get in between the cars? Why didn't someone honk their horn? I remember my wife even saying that she had dropped the dish out of her lap, and as she bent down to pick it up, that the car made a complete circle, right in the middle of the freeway. Now how can that be? I have finally come to the conclusion, and I believe with all my heart, as strange as it may seem, that God, in some miraculous way, stopped time and transported our car from one location to another. What even seems to be more amazing is that this car which almost hit us was nowhere to be found. I remember driving all the way home, approximately 20 miles, traffic never changing once, weeping over and over. I just couldn't stop.

When I arrived home, I instantly went and picked up a Bible, and it opened exactly to Matthew chapter 6. It was talking about entering into the closet, and without even thinking, I felt led to do something I had never done before: enter the closet. As I walked into the closet, I felt such an overwhelming Presence, that it just drove me to my knees. I don't remember kneeling that long, but out of nowhere appeared this vision. It was Jesus, and He was crying in a garden. Without realizing it, I spoke up and said, "Lord, why are You crying?" And from within my spirit, He started talking to me and said, "Because there is one whom I have called, but because of who he believes he is, he doesn't believe he can be used." I said, "Lord, something happened to me. Tell me who it is, I'll go tell them." And he said, "I can't do that." and I replied, "Well, why not?" and he said, "Because I'm talking to him." I was so stunned that I started weeping and laughing all at the same time. I said, "Do you know who you are talking to?" For even though I could read and write, I couldn't comprehend anything after I'd read it. I said, "This is a joke, right?" Then He said, "I'm going to take you in front of tens, and hundreds, and thousands, and even greater." I proceeded to get up and walk right out of the closet.

You know, God wouldn't quit bothering me. The first thing I noticed coming out of the closet was a small pocket Bible on the end of our bed. Now I'll tell you, that Bible was not there when I entered the closet. I picked up the Bible, opened it, and instantly threw it on the bed, for I couldn't believe what I had just seen. Every word in that Bible was written in huge bold letters. Finally, I decided once again to pick up that Bible, and would you believe it? The very first page I turned to was Matthew 26:39-40. You know what it was talking about? Jesus praying in the garden! It was the actual vision I had just seen in the closet a few moments before. Was God trying to get my attention or what?

I remember the Spirit spoke to me very clearly and said, "Terry, can you now watch with me one hour?" For He had gone to the church (Peter, James, and John), and what did they do? They slept. At a time when He needed someone, He found no one. So, beloved, the question now becomes, what are you going to do about it? Are you going to be like Peter, James, and John, or are you going to begin and take immediate action?

For you see, without a doubt, your prayer time has got to become the most important time in your everyday walk. Not only should it be a time of peace and enjoyment, but it is even more exciting to know that as you come before Him, He actually does show up, and He wants to spend time just with you, alone, getting to know your heart.

Probably one of the most difficult times for me was listening to the Spirit, learning that it wasn't just about meeting my needs nor what He could do for me, but realizing what could I do for Him. Looking back now, I realize that I didn't understand how to pray. It was going to take time to develop, and as for me, that it did. For I became so consumed in my prayer time that I spent over 13 years, seven days a week, wherever I was, in a closet a minimum of one hour a day, if not more.

At this time, I would like to take a few moments to share with you what He taught me regarding prayer and still does to this day. First, there's never a time I approach Him that I don't always begin by saying, "Father, I just praise you and thank you, right now, for this glorious opportunity you have given me to come and enter into Your presence. What a joy it is that as I come before you, to know that you truly do want to spend time with me, your son, Terry, as well as You would with any other family member, son or daughter. And Lord, I thank you that I don't enter into a realm made by the hands of man, but I enter into a realm where there is no doubt, no fear, no unbelief, no poverty, no sickness, but only one of love, joy, peace, and kindness. For not only have I been made acceptable and have access to Your presence, but I have the right to come before you because I have been made a joint heir. Everything that has been given unto Jesus has been given unto me. I lack in nothing, but have been made complete, according to Colossians 2:10."

In Matthew 6:33, this passage is talking about learning that God is a God of order, and for you to become a person of order, that it's just not going to be enough to *talk* about doing it. You are going to have to prove your loyalty, and you will do so by the manner in which you come before Him as it is spoken of in Ephesians chapter 6: with the breastplate of righteousness, the helmet of salvation, shield of faith, sword of the Spirit, your loins girded with truth, and your feet shod with the gospel of peace. By coming before Him dressed appropriately, you are showing that your purpose in coming is not as one who comes to receive, but as one who comes to serve. For the person who comes to serve is going to be the one to receive, because he proves it by the manner in which he comes dressed.

Now please don't misunderstand what I'm about to say. For

such a long time, I felt that the real key to victorious Christian living was just believing in His Word. And, yes, there is much truth in that statement, for it is the answer which the Lord has given unto a dying world. But then the Spirit spoke to me and said, "Terry, what good does it do for you to believe in My Word if you can't be trusted to do something with it? For if the words just stay on the page, then tell me, what have you accomplished?"

When it comes to your needing God to do something in your life, you will just about fight anyone to be first in line, but when it comes to Him trusting you

to spend time with Him in prayer,
to spend time with Him in His Word,
to spend time with Him in meditation,
to spend time with Him in memorizing,
to spend time with Him in witnessing,

you are nowhere to be found.

So, child of God, I beg of you, don't let it almost take an accident in your life to make you realize the importance of the urgency of the moment, but learn that the Lord is looking for that one who will come before Him with boldness, as in Hebrews 4:16,

Let us therefore come boldly unto the throne of grace, that we may obtain mercy, and find grace to help in time of need.

Realize in your heart that it is not just about praying words, but it is about learning the importance of praying the Word (John 15:7).

The Urgency of the Moment

If ye abide in me, and my words abide in you, ye shall ask what ye will, and it shall be done unto you.

By praying the Word, you are praying the answer, you are praying the solution, you are building the temple within you, and it is not upon sinking sand, but it is established (set upon a firm foundation).

So do you really expect me to believe you're doing your very best, that there's nothing else you can do? And you know what, you can tell me you are, and I'll believe you. But I'm not the one you have to convince. So, are you really sure? Really? For I just thought I'd let you know, your flood gates are open, and you know, I believe I hear an urgent cry.

So toiler, attention! Your moment is here. Build, build, build, build, build.

Epilogue

I find it extremely difficult to bring this whole topic to a close, especially when I find that there is so much more left to be said. My only desire is that you begin to have that joy of building your temple within yourself, as Nehemiah, Habakkuk, and Ezra did. For it seemed they just couldn't wait to have fellowship with their Father. Once again, I want to challenge you never come to a place where you believe you have done all you can do or have said all you can say. For you are going to find that the joy of building your temple is not in starting, but in realizing that there never is an ending, that it is an everyday, ongoing process, not just for you, or that lost soul, but also for a fellow believer who, at times, finds the way so difficult.

Philippians 1:27 says,

Only let your conversation be as it becometh the gospel of Christ: that whether I come and see you, or else be absent, I may hear of your affairs, that ye stand fast in one spirit, with one mind striving together for the faith of the gospel....